HOW TO FIND YOUR
DREAM DOG
DIXIE TENNY

Photography by Lynn Terry of Lynn Terry Photography

A Master Wordsmith Book

THE
MASTER WORDSMITH
Masterpiece Services for Entrepreneur Authors

www.themasterwordsmith.com

Published by Authors Unite

www.authorsunite.com

TABLE OF CONTENTS

INTRODUCTION

So you've decided to adopt a dog. How exciting! What kind?

The cute kind? Wait, all puppies are cute! But will you choose a puppy, or maybe an adolescent dog, or an adult? Will your new dog be big, medium, small, or, with a mixed-breed puppy, a bit of a surprise? Long hair, short hair, curly hair, wiry hair, no hair? Protective, or a social butterfly? Funny and goofy, or serious-natured? Very active, moderately active, a couch potato?

Hold on a minute, I hear you say. Why do I have to answer all these questions? It's just a dog! Why can't I just go out and pick up a dog, any dog? A dog is a dog is a dog, right?

Well, actually...

Every dog is different. And not just in size, or fur, or the shape of their ears. Every dog is right for a different owner. The best dog for me may not be the best dog for you, and neither of our dogs might be the perfect pet for someone else.

Let's look at an example.

Family A's two children, ages four and six, had been pestering their parents for a puppy for months. Their parents didn't really want a dog but felt that it might be good for teaching the children responsibility. On Christmas morning, the parents presented the children with a wiggly lab mix pup they had gotten from a shelter the day before. There had only been one young puppy at the shelter, so although the parents had hoped for something small and quiet, they reluctantly took what was available.

The children were thrilled at first. Then the puppy started jumping on them and licking their faces while they were trying to open their other presents. The more they pushed the puppy down, the more he jumped back up. When he wasn't jumping on them, he was exploring, chewing on wrapping paper and presents, and piddling on the carpet.

Finally, the pup was shut into the bathroom, where he barked and scratched the door nonstop for fifteen minutes. He must be hungry, the parents thought, and left the Christmas morning festivities to feed the puppy. When they opened the door they saw that paint was scratched off it and that there was poop smeared all over the floor, none of it anywhere near the newspaper they had laid out.

They took the puppy to the kitchen and while they were pouring his food into his bowl, he piddled again. He ate his food, and then pooped on the kitchen floor.

By this time the puppy stank of poo and the children ran screaming from the stinky pup. He gleefully chased after them all over the house, leaving poo paw prints all over the carpet. When he caught up to the four-year-old, he jumped on her back and knocked her down. As she screamed and cried, the parents deposited the puppy back into the bathroom. The next day, they returned the puppy to the shelter.

How to Find Your Dream Dog

Two days later Family B arrived at the shelter. They hoped to adopt a puppy when they still had a few days of vacation to help him settle in. They were an active family with two pre-teen children and wanted a pup who could grow up to hike and camp with them. Their research indicated that a lab or lab mix would be a good choice. They had checked the shelter over Thanksgiving vacation but didn't find a good candidate. This time they saw the puppy that Family A had returned.

They took the lab puppy to the shelter's Get-Acquainted room and spent half an hour getting to know him. He was high-energy, but their calm behavior calmed him as well. They ignored his jumping up until he stopped jumping, petting him only when he stayed on all fours. Soon he wasn't jumping up at all. He loved lying on his back on the daughter's lap as she gently scratched his chest. They had brought some treats along, and found that this smart fellow could be easily guided to sit or lie down for a goodie. With the training to focus on, he became steady and responsive. They decided this was the pup for them and adopted him.

When the family got home, the children watched the puppy in their yard while their parents got the pup's area ready for him. The pup did his business, and the children played a game where they called him back and forth, crouching down so he didn't jump up, and rewarding him with a cuddly scratch-fest each time he arrived. When their parents called them inside, they carried the pup to the kitchen, which had been gated off. A heavy water bowl and half a dozen toys of different kinds were set up on the floor.

The pup joyfully began to romp, play, and chew. Since he was very young and his day had been exciting already, he began to slow down after about ten minutes of play. Since the kids and their dad were in the kitchen watching him, they noticed as soon as the puppy's energy dropped. They took him back outside, where he immediately piddled. Back in the kitchen, the pup carried a chew toy to a soft towel and laid down to chew. Within two minutes he was sound asleep.

The family named their puppy Clark, after Clark Kent, because although he looked like an ordinary lab mix, they knew he was going to grow up to be a superdog.

Clark the lab puppy was a disaster for Family A, and the perfect puppy for Family B. The same dog, two completely different outcomes. Why?

I'll give you a hint: it didn't have anything to do with Clark himself.

The successful adoption of a puppy (or any age dog) begins with you. Puppies are not blank slates. There are wonderful puppies out there for almost all individuals and families. But as we see in the case of Family A and Family B, the same puppy isn't right for everyone.

This book will position you to be Family B - to find the right puppy, or dog, that will become a beloved part of your family.

First, we will look at everything that needs to be considered before you decide to adopt a puppy or a new adult dog. What did Family A do wrong? What did Family B do right? How can you, too, be successful from the very beginning?

Next, we will look at the process of choosing a puppy or dog. How do you know what type of puppy will be right for you? How do you choose the best individual for you from a litter? And is it possible that you might want to consider adopting an adolescent or adult dog instead?

Finally, we will consider all the ways you might acquire your puppy, from the promising to the potentially disastrous.

Most people spend hours researching a new mattress, days researching a new car, and weeks, months, even years researching a new home or new job. The time you spend finding the right item or situation is vital, because it will be part of your life for years to come. Yet almost no one spends more than a few minutes—long enough to look up the address of the nearest pet shop or shelter—researching the right canine companion for the next ten-to-fifteen years of their life. So like family A, they get a dog, any dog, and more often than not they don't keep it.

Every dog (other than the young puppies) that you see in a shelter is there because it was someone's wrong choice.

This doesn't have to happen. I don't want it to happen to any dog or any owner. I don't want it to happen to you. Each of those dogs is still the right choice for someone. One of them might be right for you. If not, we can find the dog who is.

This book will help match you with your Dream Dog, a dog that will be a joy for you from the day it arrives in your home until the end of its life. It contains everything I've learned in more than thirty years of working with dogs and owners: the most and least successful reasons to get a dog; how to figure out what kind of dog is best for you; how to find that dream dog and bring it home. Since the majority of owners start with a puppy (and puppies require the most work), much of the book focuses only on puppies, but the final section takes the same principles and applies them to getting an adolescent or adult dog.

I've seen hundreds of families successfully adopt and form lifetime bonds with amazing dogs by following the practices in these pages. You, too, can find the dog of your dreams, one who is and will remain physically, mentally, and emotionally stable, and one who will always be "the best dog ever" until the end of its days.

Let's get you ready for your Dream Dog!

Dixie Tenny

PART 1:
Getting Ready For Your Dream Dog

Do you REALLY want a puppy?

"Of course I do!" you may be thinking. "I'm reading this book, aren't I?" And you may be right. But asking if you want a puppy isn't like asking if you want a new TV. It's a lot more complicated.

For one thing, young puppies are very similar to crawling babies. Both learn about the world by exploring everything in reach and by putting things in their mouths. Neither arrives house trained or able to communicate. Neither understands "appropriate" behavior, and both will make a lot of mistakes as they learn it. Both need constant supervision and care during the earliest stages of their lives. Both require financial output, time, and attention from you—whether you feel like giving it or not. And neither will grow up to be a calm, relaxed adult without thoughtful guidance from you while they're young.

Here are some helpful questions you can ask yourself to determine if you really want a puppy:

- Are you willing to decide on the best type of puppy for you and your lifestyle, and then wait for that puppy, if necessary?

- Can you resist cute puppies that are not likely to grow into the right kind of dog for you until the right one does come along?

- Every puppy will need a great deal of your time and attention for the first six to twelve weeks of its life with you, even when you are tired, busy, sick, or don't feel like it. It will continue to need daily time, attention, supervision, and guidance until it is approximately 18 months old. How much time and energy do you have to give a puppy? Are you ready to make that degree of commitment?

- Do you understand and accept everything that is part of a normal puppy's behavior? Are your expectations of a young puppy realistic? Will you educate yourself about kind, humane ways to modify or redirect those behaviors so that they mostly occur when and where you want them to? (Hint: the Resources list in the back of this book can help!)

- If you want a dog for your children, do you also want one for yourself?

Keep your answers to these questions in mind as we go along. See how you feel by the end of the book.

Here's one more question: *why* do you want a puppy?

Do you want a furry friend to cuddle with? A guard for your home? A playmate for your kids? A cute "child" that you can be parent to without totally giving up your life? An exercise partner? A responsibility lesson for an older child? A companion to grow with you?

Some of those reasons are great. Some of them are not. In the next chapter, we'll look at some common reasons people get puppies or adopt dogs—from the puppy's perspective as well as our own—and see how some reasons are much better than others.

1 Why I (Think I) Want a Puppy!

There are lots of different reasons people want a puppy. Let's look at several of these reasons and consider whether we think they will result in a happy outcome for people and pup.

Reason 1: So the puppy can grow up with the kids

Young children and puppies seem like a magical combination. TV is constantly showing us advertisements where happy children run in a field with a puppy at their heels, babies and puppies are cuddling, or kids and dogs are getting into adorable mischief together.

But if the camera ran a little longer, we might get to see a different side to children and puppies: the one where the cuddling puppy starts chewing on the baby's fingers and the baby starts to scream; where the puppy catches up to the running children and jumps on them, knocking them to the ground; where a tired and harried parent with no tolerance for mischief, however cute, shouts at the child and the puppy, sending the child to his room and dumping the puppy outside.

Puppies and young children can have wonderful moments together, if they are carefully monitored. But puppies, like toddlers, want to be in motion every waking moment. And for baby dogs, that means exploring the environment, including human skin, with their teeth. It means running and jumping, digging and chewing, tugging and growling, until they collapse into sleep.

Few parents of young children ever say "I wish I had another young child to take care of!" Yet for the first months of a puppy's life with its family, the family basically has another toddler. Puppies must be supervised every waking moment, and when you also have a child who fits that description, you have just doubled up on your job as a parent. Remember what happened in puppy Clark's first home, with Family A? That wasn't an exaggeration. That's exactly what happens to unprepared families who adopt a puppy while they have young children.

Would you be prepared to care for an additional small child for a month or two? If not, think seriously before you get a puppy.

Reason 2: For my (older) child who desperately wants her own puppy

What about a child old enough to care for a puppy herself? The responsible preteen girl or boy who has nothing on their birthday list except a puppy?

This can work, but only if the parents know that no matter how much the child longs and begs for a puppy, no child should ever be expected to be solely responsible for the lifetime of the dog.

A child of ten or eleven is not capable of understanding what it means to make a twelve- to seventeen-year commitment to a social animal who needs daily interaction to stay healthy and happy.

First of all, does the child want the dog as much as she wants the puppy? A puppy only stays little and cute for a month or two before turning into a gangly adolescent and then an adult dog. If the child is in love with puppies, getting one will only satisfy her for the very short time before the puppy begins to grow up.

Secondly, a child won't really understand what it takes to take care of a puppy—they've never done it. Saying "you do realize it will be your job to take this puppy outside whenever it needs to go, to keep it from chewing things up, to take it for walks and to puppy classes, to train it to be a great dog…" is unrealistic. Of course any child who wants a

How to Find Your Dream Dog

puppy will nod vigorously and insist that she will do all those things — but she has no frame of reference for what that will actually mean. She will likely do her best, but you, the parent, will be the one who will need to pick up the slack if and when she forgets or doesn't follow through.

Thirdly, puppies and young dogs need constant supervision. Who will care for the puppy-then-dog while the child owner is at school, doing homework, at sleepovers, away at camp, or attending after-school and weekend sports practice and events? That adds up to a lot of hours when someone else is going to need to feed, exercise, train, and play with the child's puppy/dog.

And finally, whatever you longed for when you were eleven, was that the same thing you continued to wish for with all your heart when you were thirteen? Sixteen? Nineteen? A young dog that was desperately wanted as a puppy may find itself upstaged by a growing child's social life, extracurricular activities, dates, etc. Yet the dog still has the same daily needs for attention and care. The average lifespan of a dog is 12-15 years. That eleven-year-old child will be off to work or college, possibly in another town, possibly even starting a family of his own by the time that puppy grows old.

If your older child loses interest, are you ready and willing to step in to raise, care for, and love the dog?

Reason 3: My wonderful dog was important to me growing up, and I want my children to have that experience too.

This can be fine. But keep in mind that 1) your children are not you, and 2) it's unlikely that you were the person actually raising that childhood puppy you remember. Your parents, and maybe older siblings, did a lot of that work for you— you were just too young to notice.

Be sure your children actually want a family dog. They may not be as interested as you, or they might be too busy to enjoy the new puppy for more than occasionally.

And that wonderful dog you remember from your childhood? Someone went to the trouble to raise and train a puppy so that it became that wonderful dog. In this case, that person will be you. Do you have the extra time and energy in your life for this project? And the knowledge to do it properly? High hopes and happy memories are not what it takes to create a great family dog. It takes education, a great deal of time and work, and lots of patience.

Reason 4: I need to get more exercise. If I have a dog, I'll walk it every day and get healthier.

Getting a puppy in the hopes that it will force you to be more active is not fair to the dog and unrealistic for most people. If you want to exercise with a new dog, try developing a new walking schedule on your own first. See how long you keep it up, and how much you enjoy it. Some people do find they enjoy new exercise routines, but many more struggle to maintain them and revert to their old, sedentary behaviors very quickly. A dog will not make you want to exercise if you don't already want to—you may even come to resent a high-energy dog that needs to be walked all the time.

A dog is not a treadmill. You can't just use it for a while, decide you don't feel like using it after all, and consign it to the basement. A dog is a living being with daily needs that must be met, regardless of whether it is meeting your needs or not.

Be aware: a puppy will not be a suitable distance-walking or running partner until it is grown. Puppies can suffer serious, permanent damage to their bodies if they are made to over-exercise while they are still growing. In general, a dog should be about a year old before it starts exercising with you, depending on the individual. It's essential to have a veterinarian check your dog for physical soundness before you do any vigorous exercise with him; if he has any orthopedic issues such as hip, elbow, or shoulder dysplasia, exercise can make those problems much worse. And always build up your dog's exercise slowly and gradually, just as a human would need to do.

It's not easy to find a good canine walking or running partner. Some dog breeds are unsuited for running at all, others have difficulty breathing if walked too far or too fast, and many have gaits different enough from the human walk or jog that moving at our pace is difficult or painful. We'll talk more about which breeds are good exercise partners when we talk about choosing the right dog for you.

Finally, training a dog to walk or run comfortably with a person while ignoring oncoming people and other dogs generally requires the help of a competent professional and a long learning period before both owner and dog are happy and comfortable. And although a dog may eventually learn to walk or run alongside a person, that is not a dog's preferred way of "taking a walk." Dogs want to stop and sniff interesting places. Be sure your canine partner gets some amble-and-sniff time along with the exercise.

Reason 5: I really want a puppy, I know I have the time and energy to raise one, and I am eager to learn what I need to know to choose one wisely, so that the puppy joining my home will grow into a dog I will keep and love all its life.

This is the best, and I might even say the only, reason to get a puppy. You need to really want a dog, because that dog is going to need a great deal of your attention and take up a great deal of your time (a puppy much more than an adult dog, but all dogs need time and attention).

According to Seattle Purebred Dog Rescue, the #1 reason owners give up their pets isn't a behavior issue. It's "no time for the dog." Examine your life now, honestly, and be realistic. Do you have the time to raise a puppy into a great dog?

And it's so important to choose the right puppy or dog. Any dog trainer will tell you that many so- called "behavior problems" are caused by a mismatch between owner and dog. "My dog needs more exercise than I can give it." (Then why did you choose a young Labrador Retriever mix?) "My dog pulls like crazy on walks." (A Siberian Husky mix wasn't the best choice if you wanted to avoid pulling.) "My dogs fight all the time." (Getting female terrier littermates made this a likely outcome.) The right dogs for those owners were out there, but the owners didn't have the knowledge they needed to make the best choices for themselves and their dogs. They acquired their dogs impulsively, without consulting experts, doing research, or planning for success.

2 Do You Have What It Takes To Be A Great Dog Owner?

So you've examined your reasons for wanting a puppy and decided they are the right ones. That's a great start! But having your heart in the right place isn't all that's needed. In the next chapter, we'll look at everything—absolutely everything—you'll need to have, do, be, and know to be a great puppy and dog owner.

So now you know a puppy is probably right for you. But are you right for a puppy? That's not as easy as it sounds. Simply wanting the puppy, no matter how sure you are that you do want it, isn't enough to guarantee that you'll have a good experience and a happy, healthy dog. There's a lot more needed to be truly ready to become a successful dog owner.

To succeed in raising a puppy into a wonderful dog, you will need the following:

1. Time

Your new dog will need a great deal of your time, especially if you get a young puppy. In its first few months with you, you will literally need to be aware of where your puppy is and what he is doing every moment of the day. Remember, an 8-week-old puppy is similar in many ways to a crawling baby without a diaper on. Would you leave that baby unsupervised? Astonishingly, many owners do just that with their young puppies, and then feel angry and surprised to find items chewed and accidents on the carpet. Young puppies, just like crawling babies, need supervision 100% of the time, unless they are resting in a safe and secure confined space such as a crate or an exercise pen (the equivalents of a crib and playpen for a baby).

The need for very intense supervision lasts for the first two or three months that a puppy spends in its new home. And the growing young dog will continue to need supervision when people are home and confinement when they are not until he is about 18 months old. Yes, that seems like a very long time. But young dogs left unsupervised too soon develop habits such as furniture-chewing, repetitive barking, and counter-surfing. Dogs who do not have those opportunities when they are young seldom if ever develop those habits during their adult lives.

Another important way your puppy will need your time, from his arrival in your home to the age of about 16 weeks, is for socialization outings. A puppy needs to be socialized so it gets used to the world. This socialization period is crucial to the puppy's development, as it determines how the puppy views what is safe vs. what is scary for the rest of its life. The pup must be carefully exposed to all the things it will be expected to react to calmly during the rest of its life. You, the owner, must take the puppy out into the world almost every day during those weeks, and orchestrate the outings so that they are positive events for the puppy. The goal of socialization is for your puppy to build good associations with riding in a car, meeting strangers, being around children, passing by other dogs calmly, hearing the hiss of buses and the wail of sirens, feeling grass and gravel and wood chips under his feet, smelling city smells and country smells, and so much more. This must happen at this stage in your puppy's life no matter what season you get him in, something to consider if you have brutally hot summers or frigid winters.

There is no way to overemphasize how important this socialization period is. A puppy who spends this entire period in someone's backyard will never be relaxed and comfortable going for walks or interacting civilly with strangers. He will never take new experiences in his stride. He is unlikely to be safe with children or strangers, although that may not be apparent until he matures. The unfortunate truth is that a puppy who is not properly socialized before the age of 16-18 weeks may not ever be a good family pet.

Do you have the time to properly socialize a puppy for the first two months he is living with you, and to supervise him carefully for the first year?

2. Money

Whether you buy a pricey purebred or adopt a "free" puppy from the family down the street, pet ownership is not cheap. Puppies need a series of vaccinations in their early months in order to be protected against common diseases, then occasional vaccinations throughout their adult lives. Good quality puppy food helps the puppy develop well physically and can prevent issues such as chronic diarrhea or skin allergies that dyes and fillers in cheap foods can cause. Crates, baby gates, exercise pens, leashes, collars, identification tags, microchips, bowls, toys, treats — these are all basic items a puppy needs and the costs add up. Most will need spay/neuter surgery at some point. And of course, accidents happen, so be prepared to pay emergency veterinary bills. You won't spend quite as much on a puppy as on a human child—but it might seem that way sometimes.

3. Energy

Can you keep up with a young puppy? During puppyhood and most of a dog's first year, awake = on the move, running and jumping and playing nonstop until they fall asleep again. And they will not be able to sleep through the night for the first few weeks, so you will need to find the energy to have your sleep interrupted once or twice (or more) to take the puppy outdoors.

4. Knowledge

Humans don't instinctively know how to build great relationships with dogs. Many of us have never watched anyone else successfully raise a puppy. Even if we had a puppy as a child, we may not remember what it took to raise it from puppy to dog. This lack of knowledge can damage what could otherwise be a wonderful relationship between owner and dog.

Most people consult experts when making major purchases and investments. Strangely, very few people do this when choosing a companion dog to be part of their family for a decade or more. Research tells us that most prospective puppy-buyers consult no one before purchasing a puppy; not even a veterinarian, a pet supply store employee, or a neighbor with a dog, let alone an actual expert.

Family A's puppy-buying experience was a disaster and a failure. Why? Because they thought they would figure out how to handle a puppy on the fly. They went out and impulsively adopted the first available puppy, which happened to be a poor choice for their family, and brought it home having acquired no knowledge about how to raise it and having made no preparations for its arrival.

Many people put much more time, thought, and research into choosing a car, a house, a school for their children, a

How to Find Your Dream Dog

mutual fund, an insurance policy, even a mattress than they do a puppy.

The good news is that we live in an age where scientifically valid and helpful information is readily available. It's not hard to learn to do the right things, especially once you know how to sift through the misinformation and find the good stuff. The resource list at the back of this book can help you do that. But you have to actually do the research and acquire the knowledge before your puppy arrives. What you don't know can and will hurt both you and your puppy-to-be.

5. Patience

It may come as a surprise to many first-time dog owners, but puppies are not born understanding human language. They learn the meaning of words the same way human babies do: by patient repetition, pairing word with object or action.

No one rushes babies when it comes to learning language. But people seem to think that puppies are born understanding the word "no" and will respond to every other word they are told after hearing it just once or twice. Nothing you do can make a puppy learn faster than its natural development allows it to. As with a baby or toddler, you must be prepared to spend months patiently teaching your puppy everything you want it to know, and understand that there will be many missteps along the way. Being prepared to face even the most frustrating mistakes with love and patience is an important part of being ready for a puppy.

6. Everyone else in your family on board with you

Unless you're single and live alone, you aren't the only one who will interact with this puppy on a daily basis. Does everyone in your family want a puppy? Is everyone willing to be patient and consistent with treatment, vocabulary, and training? Puppies are a constant, active presence in a household. It is not fair to the puppy to bring it into a home where someone does not want it, or where someone will sabotage the careful raising and training being done by the rest of the family. So if you live with others, talk frankly together about these issues.

Here are some questions to consider with your family, roommates, and/or live-in partner:

- Have everyone's preferences been taken into account so that the new arrival can be as close as possible to the whole family's dream dog?

- Who will be the main caretaker for the puppy? That person needs to be enthusiastically on board in order for this to be successful.

- If there are children in the family, what role will they play in caring for the puppy? Are the adults willing to step in when the children are busy or lose interest?

- Are there regular visitors, such as elderly relatives, dog-allergic individuals, or families with babies or toddlers, that

How to Find Your Dream Dog

you need to consider? What about the neighbors? It's your puppy, but if they're anti-dog, it could be a problem.

- Does your family have other pets? How will you bring a puppy into their space and ensure harmony?

Whew! Okay, I know that's a lot to think about and discuss. But if you consider carefully and decide that you do have all six of these areas covered, then chances are excellent that you can adopt and raise a happy, well-adjusted puppy.

Now let's zoom out and take a wider view of preparation for a puppy. There are some things that all dogs and puppies will do. Not every dog will do every action, but puppies will do most of them, so be ready for them all.

For all their many differences, all dogs have a lot in common.

3 Normal Behaviors of Puppies and Dogs

Here are some behaviors that you will see with any and every dog:

- Barking

- Growling

- Chewing

- Biting

- Digging

- Running

- Jumping

- Urinating and defecating

- Vomiting

- Helping themselves to any food they can reach (aka "counter-surfing")

- Rolling on the ground

- Walking through mud

- Shaking themselves off when wet, wherever they happen to be
- Chasing anything moving fast

Many dogs will also do some or all of the following:

- Howling
- Fixating on a caged bird, hamster, or other small pet
- Chasing small animals and killing them if they can catch them
- Shredding paper and other objects
- Disemboweling soft toys
- Eating poop and vomit
- Rolling in smelly dead things

The items in these lists are simply normal dog traits. They are part of the package labeled "Dog," just as talking, blowing our noses, needing to use the toilet several times every day, walking upright, and laughing are part of the package labeled "Human."

How would you feel if someone tried to stop you from doing any of those normal human behaviors? Yet owners often express a wish to "stop the dog from barking" or "stop the dog from chewing things" and so on. Normal behaviors should not be shut down, but they can be managed. Your job is to teach your puppy or dog when and where to perform each of those behaviors, and to manage the environment so behavior you do not want cannot happen. For example, if you don't want your dog to tear apart soft toys, give him tear-resistant toys without stuffing, hard rubber toys, and/ or other safe alternatives to "stuffies." You can also avoid behaviors you don't want by training alternate behaviors. A dog who is lying on a mat in the kitchen can't be counter-surfing for goodies.

Remember, it will be your job to supervise or humanely confine your pup whenever he is awake until he is mature enough and educated enough to make the correct choices and behave appropriately. As I mentioned earlier, you must be willing to teach your puppy kindly and patiently, as you would a crawling baby. *Always remember that what is normal behavior for dogs is not, in most cases, normal behavior for us, and vice versa.*

Sadly, many people raise their puppies using much harsher methods than they would ever use with their babies. Rather than addressing mistakes with patience, kindness, and gentle teaching, many owners punish their puppies, as if somehow these baby animals arrived in the house knowing the difference between right and wrong, and chose to do wrong on purpose.

The puppy in this situation has no idea why he is being punished, only that he has left the warmth and security of his mother and littermates to land in a place where his normal puppy behaviors may be met with encouragement, may be ignored, or may cause punishment. One example is jumping up on an owner's leg, something puppies naturally do. Sometimes jumping may be encouraged (owner thinks puppy is cute and cuddles it). Sometimes it gets ignored (owner is on the phone and turns away). And sometimes it is punished (owner is wearing dress clothes and kicks the puppy away).

Not only does this confuse the puppy, it also frightens him, since he never knows if he might be punished for doing something that comes naturally to him. And if punishment continues, the puppy is likely to become defensive and may snap or bite. It is very hard for love and loyalty to grow in an atmosphere of punishment and fear. How would you feel about working for a boss who seemed to always be looking for reasons to punish you? How about one whose relationship with you was like a mentor's, based on guidance and praise?

Why do so many people yell at and smack their puppies? Because, frankly, it is a lot easier than taking the time and energy necessary to guide them through puppyhood kindly and thoughtfully. Also, punishment is rewarding to the punisher. It relieves our anger to shout or smack. The puppy runs away, looking guilty, and we have the additional relief of thinking "I hated to do that, but it did the job."

But the fact is that the only thing the punishment truly accomplished was to make your puppy begin to fear you. What appears to be a look of guilt on a dog's face is actually a look of appeasement, saying "please don't yell at/hurt me anymore." A dog who is yelled at or smacked for doing a normal dog behavior does not understand why that happened any more than you would understand someone walking up and smacking you for sneezing, brushing your hair, or doing any other normal human behavior.

If a behavior was done in the wrong place or at the wrong time — an accident on the rug, the television remote being chewed, your child's shoe proudly carried in from his bedroom — the puppy is not the one who made a mistake. Your puppy or dog is telling you he is not far enough along in his development or his learning to make the right choices yet. To help him learn the right choices in a supportive environment, a puppy or a dog new to a household should always be in one of the following three situations:

- Actively supervised by a responsible person, indoors or out.

- Actively engaged, learning correct behaviors through play.

- Humanely confined in a crate, exercise pen, or safe room behind a baby gate.

Would you start a work project on your computer with a crawling baby unsupervised in the house? Of course not. Leaving a puppy or untrained young dog, or any dog new to a household, loose in the house can result in accidents, tooth marks on chair legs, and even injury to the dog from chewing an electrical cord or swallowing Legos. So while you're supervising this new puppy, you aren't just training and socializing it. You're also making sure it stays safe.

To finish out this section, let's take a closer look at what that supervision looks like by examining daily life with a young puppy.

4 A Day In The Life

Puppies, like crawling babies, are little nonstop exploring machines. Very young puppies (under approximately 12 weeks) cannot be expected to sleep through the night without at least one potty break, often more at first. An average 24 hours with an 8-week-old puppy usually looks something like this:

12am: Take whining puppy out of his crate and carry him outside to potty, then return him to his crate. Attempt to sleep.

4am: Repeat.

6-7am: Take whining puppy outside to potty, then to the kitchen to feed him breakfast. He eats, drinks, then must go outside to potty again. Sit on the floor and play with puppy for 10-15 minutes, then outside to potty again. Puppy chews on toys in the gated kitchen while you prepare your own breakfast. After

How to Find Your Dream Dog

10-15 minutes, puppy looks for a place to sleep. You gently move puppy to crate at 8:30am. He fusses for a minute or two and then settles.

10:30am: Puppy wakes and whines. You take puppy outside to potty. Puppy has access to water (all the time when in the kitchen play area). Puppy drinks, then plays for about ten minutes and begins to circle. You quickly take puppy outside and he potties. You play outdoors with the puppy, he eventually potties again. You bring him inside, he chews on toys and plays.

12pm: You give him his second meal of the day. He eats, drinks, and needs to go outside to potty. Once back inside, he plays very briefly and then looks for a place to sleep. You put him into his crate at 12:45pm.

3pm: Puppy wakes and whines; you take him outside to potty. You put the puppy in his crate in the car and drive to your children's school. You sit on a bench near the playground with the puppy on your lap for fifteen minutes so he can see and hear the activity without being too close (this is a great example of orchestrated socialization). Children who want to pet him are invited to offer him one of the treats you brought along, on a flat hand, while giving him three gentle strokes with the other hand.

3:30pm: You and your children come home from school. After the puppy potties in the front yard, the children play with the puppy in the kitchen, sitting on the floor, plush toys in their hands for puppy to chew on, always under your careful supervision. You give puppy a potty opportunity approximately every 20 minutes, watching carefully to see when he starts to sniff the floor or circle.

4:30pm: You leave puppy in the gated kitchen, having sprayed the counters at his chewing level with anti-chewing spray like Bitter Apple and supplied him with several tempting chew toys. You intend to set the children up with their homework, but you get distracted and don't return to the kitchen for 30 minutes. Puppy has had an accident. One of the children takes him outside while you clean it up thoroughly with an enzymatic cleaning solution such as Nature's Miracle. Puppy comes back inside, having pottied again outside.

5pm: Puppy gets his third meal of the day, drinks, and then goes out for another potty break. He is tired and goes into his crate on his own to sleep. You quietly latch the door.

8pm: Puppy wakes and whines in his crate. You take him outside to potty. You take some of his toys to the living room to sit on the floor and play with him during a TV show, with one eye on the show and one eye on the puppy. He makes it to the third ad break (about 45 minutes) and you realize you're pushing your luck, so you take him outside, where he immediately potties. Back inside, he plays quietly on the floor with you for another twenty minutes or so, then curls up in your lap to sleep.

10pm: You carry him outside for a last potty of the night, then put him into his crate beside your bed. He fusses for a short time and then falls asleep.

Next day: Repeat, replacing the puppy's socialization outing with a different one.

Remember how much time a young puppy will need from you? That was no exaggeration. A day in the life of a puppy is literally a 24-hour day, and you'll be on call for just about all of it. But as you can see, a regular routine can be developed when you're home with the puppy through the day. You can even get some work done while the puppy's napping.

But what about when everyone is away from the house during the day? If you're single and go to work, or both parents in a family work outside the home, your puppy will have to spend much of the day home alone. This is not ideal. Puppies are social baby animals, so it is hard on a young pup to spend so much time alone.

Your puppy will need a meal in the middle of the day until he is approximately four months old (puppies vary in how long they need this third meal; their dwindling interest in it indicates that they may be switched over to two meals a day). So someone will need to come by around lunchtime to feed the puppy.

A puppy can manage a work day alone in a long-term confinement area such as an exercise pen or a secure and puppy-proofed room as long as he gets his midday meal. His space needs to contain an assortment of safe chew toys, towels in a crate with the door removed for safety or a chew-resistant bed to nap in, water in a heavy bowl or clipped to the side of the pen so it can't be overturned, and a thick layer of newspapers completely covering the floor. If you are concerned about the floor, place a tarp under the layers of newspaper. Expect to have many accidents to clean up when you get home and possibly a puppy to wash. And remember that it is still vital that the pup gets out regularly for socialization before he reaches 16 weeks of age.

A better alternative is to find someone willing to come in to feed and play with the puppy for a while at some point during the day. A neighbor might be delighted to do this. There are professional dog sitters who can perform this task as well. You might even find someone who would be thrilled to have you drop off your puppy each work morning and pick him up again in the afternoon. The puppy would have the benefit of a different house, different people, and different experiences, the puppy sitter would have a puppy to enjoy for a few weeks, and you would have a much happier and better socialized puppy.

Puppies grow up quickly, even though those first few weeks can feel eternal. Sleep periods grow longer but there are fewer of them. The puppy's ability to control his bladder and bowels improves gradually. Eventually he will start sleeping through the night in his crate. It will be many months yet before he can safely roam the house unsupervised, but the need for 24/7 attention will drop away. Life will start to seem normal again; a new "normal," with a puppy in it.

CONCLUSION
Ready For Rover

So by this point, you should know much more clearly if you're ready to adopt and raise a puppy. Let's review:

- You feel that your reasons for wanting a puppy at this point in your life are good ones.

- You are willing to educate yourself about the best ways to raise a puppy or introduce a new dog to your household before you get one.

- You have enough time to supervise and socialize a puppy for its first 2-3 months with you.

- You have the money, energy, knowledge, and patience to support and love a new puppy.

- Your family and anyone else who will interact with the puppy are excited and ready.

How to Find Your Dream Dog

- You're familiar with the things all puppies and dogs do, and you're prepared to meet them all with patience and kindness.

- You can set up a puppy care daily schedule that works well for you and the puppy.

- You've been reading everything covered in this section and thinking "yes, yes, yes, yes, yes!"

- Or, you may be less sure that a puppy is right for you but excited about the prospect of finding the right adolescent or adult dog.

If these things are true, you're ready to find and choose your dream dog!

But which dog will that be?

The next section of this book will help you answer that question. Let's take a look at all the wonderful variety in the world of dogs.

PART 2:
Choosing Your Dream Dog

A Dog Is Not A Dog Is Not A Dog

What kind of dog will be the best pet for you? Even with all the preparation and consideration from Part 1, bringing the wrong dog into your home may well create an uncomfortable, frustrating situation for both you and the puppy. So before you can choose the puppy that will become your perfect dog, you will need to take some time to consider which of the many types of dogs you really want. How do you imagine your "dream dog"? How does it look? How does it behave?

Although many people reading this book are thinking about finding the right puppy, let us always keep in mind that you will only have a puppy for a few months, followed by many years with an adult dog. All puppies are adorable and desirable. But they grow into dogs with very different needs, looks, and personalities.

So let's stop thinking "puppy" for a few moments here and consider what kind of dog you want to live with for the next decade or two. There are all kinds of dogs, from the tiny Maltese to the huge Leonburger, from the slender Whippet to the beefy American Staffordshire Terrier, from the highly active Australian Kelpie to the mellow Clumber Spaniel.

One of the most useful places to start is with what the breed or mix of breeds you are interested in was originally bred to do. It isn't a coincidence, for instance, that Labrador Retrievers act differently from English Mastiffs. The Labrador

Retriever was designed to retrieve birds out of water after the birds had been shot by hunters. To this end, Labs have the high level of energy needed for running in the field all day, a medium-compact body size, and a water-repellent coat. Most have a passion for carrying things in their mouths, are crazy about swimming, are attentive to their owners (as they needed to be to their hunters), and do not mind doing repetitive tasks — they might have been required to retrieve many birds in a day's hunt. While there are exceptions, most Labs are generally friendly and easy-going, not suited to guard dog duty.

English Mastiffs, on the other hand, were bred primarily as property guards. They need exercise, but less than a dog bred to run in the field with a hunter all day. Since they were not required to work under the direction of a human but expected to guard an estate on their own, owners might have to work a little harder to get and keep their attention. Their great size comes with some downsides; they have a shorter life expectancy than small or medium sized dogs, and the puppies need to be supervised carefully in order to avoid injury as they grow into their big bodies. English Mastiffs can be suspicious of strangers unless well socialized to them as puppies, and are natural guard dogs.

What about mixed breed dogs? Mixed breeds are just that, a mix of breeds. Most have some identifiable breed characteristics. It is valuable to think of Labrador Retriever characteristics when considering adopting a mix that looks and acts mostly like a Labrador Retriever. The same goes

How to Find Your Dream Dog

for other mixed breeds. But since every mixed breed dog is an individual and different from all the others, sometimes no foundation breeds can be identified. In these cases, evaluate the dog on an individual basis. We'll address how to do this little further along in this book.

In the next few chapters, we will look at several factors to consider as you consider what type of dog would be best for you.

5 Energy level

Energy level is one of the most important factors to consider when looking for the right dog. You might be thrilled by the sight of a border collie leaping into the air after a Frisbee, or charmed by an English Bulldog dozing in front of a fireplace. Both are great dogs and can be perfect pets for the right owners. But if a border collie is right for you, an English Bulldog will not be, and vice versa. This is where it is very important to honestly consider your everyday life.

A border collie is one of the highest-energy breeds on earth. Imagine the energy level required to stay in control of a moving flock of sheep all day, every day. Border collies also need the high level of intelligence necessary to anticipate every move made by a flock of flighty animals, and to be able to counter those moves instantly. Taking on a border collie is a serious commitment of time and energy. Giving a border collie little or nothing to do frustrates the dog's natural drive to spend its days being busy and productive. This frustration results in "problem behaviors", which can include chewing furniture to pieces or chewing through walls, uncontrollable hyperactive behavior and/or barking, or frantic displaced "herding" behavior such as running after children and biting their heels or chasing bikes or cars. A confined border collie with no way to occupy its busy mind and body may eventually turn to self-mutilation behaviors such as chewing the skin off the backs of its own paws.

If you want a partner for high-energy dog performance activities, or herding, or to train in a variety of ways to help you around the house and yard every day, a border collie might be for you. If you're a low-key person who looks forward to quiet walks and gentle play with your dog, or who is out of the house most days and not around to engage regularly with your dog, a collie is almost surely not the dog for you.

At the other end of the spectrum, the English Bulldog is a very low-energy breed, which has also been bred with such a deformed muzzle area that it cannot breathe normally. Walking a bulldog when it is over 70F outdoors can literally kill the dog from heat prostration. Running and active play with such a dog is out of the question. This would be a disastrous breed for a prospective owner looking for a hiking companion or a competition agility dog. But bulldogs are generally easy-going and can be a fine choice for a low-energy family who enjoys quiet time at home — especially if they don't mind some snoring and slobber!

There is a wide range of energy and activity levels in dogs of all sizes. Papillons and Miniature Pinschers are active but very small; English cocker spaniels are active and medium-sized; Rhodesian Ridgebacks are active and large. Newfoundlands are very large dogs with a low activity level; Basset Hounds are low-energy and medium sized; Pekingese are small, less active dogs.

While we're talking about energy level, we also need to talk about walking (and running) with your dog. Most dogs have a natural gait that is too fast to be comfortable for people to walk along with. Many owners resort to putting a pinch or choke collar on their dogs to make them stay in position, no matter how uncomfortable that is for the dogs. Imagine being forced to walk at a pace that is not natural for you for long distances every day, with pain as the consequence of trying to slow down or speed up. If part of your new dog's life is going to be accompanying you on walks or runs, choose a type of dog with an appropriate energy level - and be prepared to engage a good trainer to help you two become real partners when you are out and about. Training a dog to walk or run comfortably with a person while also ignoring oncoming people and other dogs generally requires the help of a competent professional and a learning period.

There are some breeds well suited for long steady running, such as Dalmatians, German Shorthaired or Wire-haired Pointers, Weimaraners, and northern sledding breeds such as Siberian or Alaskan huskies. These dogs, or mixes of them, are worth consideration if you want a running partner, and if you are certain that you will actually run regularly. These breeds cannot be turned into couch potatoes if you decide that the active life is not for you. All dogs who are intended as running partners need a vet check to make sure they are physically stable enough for running, and then a program of conditioning that builds time and distance slowly.

Some dogs shouldn't be walked at all, or only very carefully. Toy dogs should never be used as exercise-walking or running partners; no matter how much they seem to dash around at home, it is cruel to force their little legs to keep up with yours out on an exercise walk. Remember, with a leash on, they have no way to stop if the walk becomes too much for them. "Brachycephalic" dogs (those with pushed-in faces, such as English bulldogs, French bulldogs, Boston terriers, and more) cannot be walked in warm weather nor should they ever be forced to walk long distances because they cannot breathe properly under those conditions. Giant breeds can walk well enough but are unsuited for running. Some other breeds, such as Basset Hounds and Dachshunds, are also unsuited for long distance walking or running. This is a topic to research before choosing the right type of dog for you, if this is one of your important issues.

So make sure you give your own energy level and exercise regimen a good hard look, and then research which types of dogs are a good fit. Your dog will thank you for giving it just the right amount of activity!

6 Attachment

When you imagine spending time with your dog at rest, is that dog in your lap, on the floor beside your chair, or across the room chewing a toy? Does it stay put no matter what, get up when you do, periodically come over to have its ears scratched, or sit at your feet, staring into your face, waiting for you to do something interesting?

In other words, how much do you want to interact with your dog when you aren't walking or playing with it? And how much physical contact do you want? Different types of dogs have very different levels of desire for physical contact.

Do you want a shadow everywhere you go? Or would you prefer a dog who is happy with an occasional pat and kind word? Some breeds, such as Chow Chows, Basenjis, and Akitas, are sometimes described as "aloof." This does not mean they are unfriendly or don't bond with their owners, just that they might not need the same amount of direct interaction or petting on a regular basis as some other types of dogs.

Other breeds are nicknamed "velcro dogs," because they prefer to be near, even touching, their owners all the time. Many Doberman Pinschers, Bernese Mountain Dogs, and Golden Retrievers are in this group. And many dogs are in between these two extremes, enjoying being stroked but also happy chewing a toy while lying near you.

As with energy level, desire to be petted and cuddled doesn't always match with the dog's size. Small terriers are busy little animals, bred to be always on the lookout for vermin to hunt and kill, and may not enjoy cuddling for extended periods of time. Then there are Irish Wolfhounds who will attempt to settle their 150 pounds onto your lap if you sit on the floor and give them the opportunity!

Think about how important it is to you to have a dog who is always happy to be stroked or held. Might it bother you to have a dog who was always sitting and leaning heavily against you at every opportunity? Or on the other hand, would your feelings would be hurt if your dog rarely (or never) wanted to cuddle with you? If a certain level of affection is important to you, make sure you choose a type of dog who will love providing it for you—and will eat it up when you return the favor.

7 Protection

Is part of this dog's job going to be to alert you to potential danger? Or even to protect you from possible harm?

Guard dogs fall into two categories — alarm dogs, whose barking can scare off intruders, and actual protection dogs, who can back up bark with bite if necessary. Even a small alarm dog is a good deterrent to crime; intruders want to break into a house in stealth and silence. Most hunting dogs, such as hounds, retrievers, setters, and spaniels, are not natural protection dogs, but they can be excellent alarm dogs. In fact, virtually all dogs will sound the alarm if they see or hear something out of the ordinary, unless they have been punished for doing so. This is natural and requires no training.

Dogs known for their protective tendencies include German Shepherds, Rhodesian Ridgebacks, Belgian Malinois, and breeds developed to guard or herd flocks, such as Great Pyrenees, Kuvasz, or Australian Cattle Dogs. Usually protection is not the only or even necessarily the primary function of breeds like these, but they do perform guard/protection behavior naturally. As for very small dogs, there have been several cases where biting Chihuahuas have thwarted attacks on their owners. So size doesn't always matter!

There are two important caveats about protection dogs.

First, while there is nothing wrong with wanting a dog who can protect you, that cannot be the only reason to get a dog. These dogs need the same attention and interaction with you as any other dog, every day. Lying around your house waiting for a possible intruder is not going to be enough for them. If you acquire a serious protection dog, be prepared to train and socialize him from puppyhood, continue socializing throughout the dog's lifetime, and possibly participate in activities such as schutzhund (a protection-related dog sport), agility, and K9 nose work to keep your smart dog mentally occupied.

These dogs tend to be medium to large, strong in body and will, and will need regular physical as well as mental exercise. They are best for experienced owners who understand the needs of their breed, and who have the time and energy to give them what they need to stay physically and mentally healthy. Please remember that any dog can give an effective alarm. Don't feel that you need to get a guard breed if all you really want is a dog who will bark if someone comes onto your property.

Second, dogs *naturally* protect their territory (house, yard, car) and the people they are bonded to. They do not need "protection training" to become effective alarm or protection dogs. Some people have the mistaken impression that the best way to create a protection dog is to isolate it from strangers, or to treat it roughly. These are not the ways to create an effective guard dog. **Those are the ways to create a *dangerous* dog.** Dogs with a natural guard instinct must be socialized very thoroughly to strangers as puppies. They need to have many good experiences with people they don't know, so that they understand that *people, in general, are not a threat.* Otherwise such a dog is a loaded gun that could go off anywhere — just as likely to attack a visiting friend or a pizza delivery person as an intruder.

This socialization will not make your dog an ineffective alarm or protection dog. Trust your dog's bond with you. He will know when someone is a threat to you, *unless you have taught him that everyone is a threat, or isolated him so that everyone is strange and scary to him.* **Please do not create a dangerous dog.**

How to Find Your Dream Dog

8 Sociability

If you are naturally a shy person, do you think someone could force you to be outgoing? If you are social and friendly with everyone, what would it take to make you shy and retiring? We know that people are born with individual personalities. These character traits are a combination of what we inherit genetically from our parents, how we are raised, and what experiences we have as we grow up.

Dogs have individual personality differences, too. While a puppy's personality is influenced by its mother and siblings, and by its experiences during its first weeks of life, there are also hard-wired differences in puppy personalities just as there are in humans. Each individual puppy in every single litter is different from its siblings, just as human siblings are often very different despite sharing the same genes and the same parents.

Some dogs respond in a friendly manner to everyone, all people, all dogs. Some love all people but only like a few dogs they know well. Others are wary of some types of people, such as children. Some dogs are not comfortable around any other dogs. Partly this is a function of the temperaments of the parent dogs, partly how well the dog was socialized during its puppyhood; also, a traumatic event could have a lifelong effect on dogs' feelings about people or other dogs. A dog of mine was jumped on during puppyhood by a well-meaning but rambunctious English Bull Terrier; my dog reacted with defensive aggression toward every other Bull Terrier he saw throughout his life. But there are also breed tendencies toward friendliness or reserve.

Learning which temperament qualities you are more likely to find in particular breeds of dogs, or in mixes of those breeds, will improve your chances of getting a dog whose level of sociability is what you are looking for.

Do you want an outgoing dog who loves everybody, gets along well with most other dogs, and is just a charmer in general? Your best chance for this type of temperament is to look at breeds that were bred to work with people and with, or in close proximity to, other dogs. Hunting dogs — retrievers, setters, spaniels, pointers, and also many hounds — and miniaturized versions of these, such as King Charles Spaniels, are often friendly with virtually everyone. Northern spitz-type breeds such as Keeshonds and Siberian Huskies are also often relaxed with other people and dogs.

Are you interested in a dog who will bond strongly with your family but won't really be interested in buddying up to strangers? Dogs whose protective instincts have been enhanced through breeding are less often immediately accepting of everyone they meet. This includes personal protection dogs such as Giant Schnauzers and Bullmastiffs, property and flock guards such as Tibetan Mastiffs, Schipperkes, and Rottweilers, and herding dogs such as Australian Shepherds and Bouvier de Flandres.

The popularity of dog parks can lead people to believe that all dogs love the company of other dogs. That is true for some dogs, but many others feel differently. Terriers, as well as some other breeds, can be feisty with other dogs. Some types of dogs are simply focused on their family and do not want to interact with other dogs. Some older, dignified dogs do not want puppies or adolescent dogs in their space. Dogs who were taken from their mothers too soon or were poorly socialized as pups can display inappropriate dog body language, which can confuse other dogs and create tense situations. Talk with experts about how the type of dog you are considering generally responds to other dogs. And if you are adopting an adolescent or adult dog from an unknown background, do not subject that dog to daycare, dog parks, or other situations where it will be forced to deal with dogs it does not know. Once you know your new dog better, you can carefully try some introductions to other dogs, ideally with the guidance of a qualified professional trainer.

Remember that as well as the tendencies of breeds and types, individual socialization makes a big difference in how dogs feel about other dogs and about people. A poorly socialized retriever is likely to be less friendly than a well-socialized mastiff. So if it's important to you that the puppy you acquire will be generally friendly, first look for a puppy in a naturally social breed or type, then follow puppy socialization guidelines very carefully.

Grooming Needs, Shedding, and Allergies

The last factor to consider has nothing to do with a dog's personality, and everything to do with its fur coat! And it's one important reason to think about the dog your puppy will become, rather than the puppy it may be now. Few young puppies need any grooming beyond nail trims and brushing. This makes it easy to forget that the darling Poodle puppy, for instance, is going to need professional grooming on a regular basis when it is an adult dog. So will the Afghan Hound, the Airedale, the Cocker Spaniel, and the Lhasa Apso, among others. The Australian Shepherd who isn't brushed regularly will develop knots of hair. The beautiful white coat of a Samoyed can mat if not groomed regularly, and can turn from white to brown after a romp in a muddy yard. Male dogs of any breed or mix with long hair on

How to Find Your Dream Dog

their stomachs will sometimes get urine on that hair when they lift their legs.

Keeping dogs of some types clean and well-groomed can be time-consuming, expensive, or both. It may be well worth the trouble for you to have such a beautiful dog... but then again, it may not. And all dogs will need some form of grooming, even if it's just a quick brush and nail trim every week.

Unless dogs exercise a great deal on a rough surface, they will all need their nails trimmed regularly. *This is not optional.* Dogs whose nails grow too long cannot walk comfortably, and eventually their feet can suffer damage. There have even been cases of dogs whose nails grew all the way around and pierced the pads of their feet. Many people are not comfortable trimming dogs' nails themselves, and many dogs are shy about having their feet handled. A good groomer can show you how to trim nails safely, or grind them with a special grinder called a dremel tool, which many dogs prefer to trimming. If you cannot trim your dog's nails, you will need to have this professionally done on a regular schedule, whether your dog needs other professional grooming or not.

Now, about shedding. Almost all dogs shed. Some, such as Golden Retrievers and German Shepherds, are notorious for leaving drifts of hair everywhere. Short-haired dogs such as Vizslas can shed just as much as long-haired ones, leaving prickly little hairs all over the furniture and the carpet. Welsh

Terriers and other wire-coated terriers do not shed, but if they are not professionally groomed ("stripped") regularly, their soft undercoat will become loose enough to stick to furniture they brush up against.

Most dog owners accept that living with dog hair is just part of dog ownership. But if that thought appalls you, consider the non-shedding breeds: all three sizes of Poodle, the Bichon Frise, the Maltese, and the wire-coated terriers are some examples. But remember, as mentioned before, these dogs have professional grooming requirements that must be fulfilled for them to remain truly non-shedding.

"Labradoodles," "Cockapoos," "Goldendoodles" and other dogs whose name ends in "- doodle" or "-poo" are cross bred between Poodles and another breed. Whether these mixed breed dogs shed or not depends on which parent's "shedding genes" are dominant in that particular dog. There can be shedders and non-shedders in the same litter. Since puppies shed very little or not at all, *there is no way to tell with these poodle mixes until they are adults whether they will shed or not.*

Finally, some people look for non-shedding breeds because of "dog allergies" in the family. Unfortunately, it is a dog's skin dander and not dog hair that triggers allergic reactions. Contrary to what many advertisements for poodle mixes claim, *there is no such thing as a hypoallergenic breed of dog.* Some dog allergy sufferers are even allergic to poodles themselves. If you very much want a dog but you or

How to Find Your Dream Dog

someone in your family has dog allergies, consider fostering a dog of the type you are considering, or "borrowing" a friend's or family member's dog, to see if the allergy sufferer has a reaction. It would be tragic for both person and dog to go through with an adoption of a dog or puppy only to find that the sufferer cannot live with the new addition to the family.

These physical factors may not seem as important as matching your dog's energy level or sociability to yours, but that doesn't mean you should ignore them! Physical attributes like grooming needs and shedding, if they aren't deal-breakers themselves, can be great deciding factors between two or more good potential dogs. A great dog with minimal grooming needs might just be a better fit than a similarly great dog that needs to be brushed every day or professionally groomed every month.

CONCLUSION

Exceptions To The Rules

This section has listed many examples of different breeds known for different personalities and behaviors. Take some time to research those examples—one of them might be exactly the dog you're looking for. If none of the examples here seem quite right for you, that's fine too. There are many more to learn about and choose from. Look through the Resources section at the end of the book for more information.

There are exceptions to all these breed generalizations. There are calm border collies, cuddly Fox Terriers, shy Brittany Spaniels, and Rottweilers who love everyone. There are dogs of all breeds whose attitudes toward humans or other dogs have been influenced by a lack of socialization, harsh training, or abusive treatment. There's no guarantee that you'll get exactly the personality you want.

How to Find Your Dream Dog

But if certain qualities are important to you, your best chance of getting what you want is to get a dog breed or similar mix known for the qualities you're looking for. Follow that up by choosing the best individual for you that you can find. Help with that is coming right up in Part 3.

So now you know you're ready for a puppy, and you have an idea of what kind of dog you want that puppy to grow into. You're finally ready to go out and find that dream puppy! Part 3 looks especially at choosing a puppy, purebred or mixed breed. Part 4 will address the option of finding the right adolescent or adult dog to adopt.

PART 3:
Finding Your Dream Puppy

Once you have decided what type of adult dog would fit well into your life, it's time to think about finding the right puppy that will grow into that adult dog.

The first thing to understand is that every puppy is different, even within the same breed, even within the same litter. Think about your children, or you and your siblings. No two individuals are the same.

There are two steps involved in finding a dream puppy. The first step is learning where to get the right kind of puppy to begin with. Then you need to discover how to choose the right individual puppy. This section will walk you through both of those steps.

10 The BEST Place To Find Purebred Puppies

The best source for a purebred puppy, hands down, is a **hobby breeder.** A hobby breeder is someone who produces puppies for love of the breed, not for profit.

Hobby breeders are dedicated to producing a line of physically, mentally, and emotionally healthy examples of their breed, where each generation improves on the last. They seldom work with more than two breeds, and most often just one. They are familiar with medical issues common to their breed(s) and perform genetic testing and health screenings to ensure that only truly sound and healthy individuals are bred.

How to Find Your Dream Dog

Hobby breeders are thorough, compassionate, and care deeply about where their puppies end up. A hobby breeder will want to meet you and your family, talk about the breed with you, and discuss your hopes and goals for your future pet. They will be glad to show you their facilities and introduce you to their adult dogs, who should be either open and friendly or calmly civil, depending on the nature of the breed. If their adults are shy, growly, or kept away from you, make your polite excuses and leave. Avoid that breeder. He might have darling puppies, but if he hides his adult dogs from you, that tells you that you are not going to find your dream dog at his facility.

Hobby breeders might have kennels, but their dogs will spend at least some time in the house. Their puppies should be born and raised in the house, so that you receive a puppy who is already used to household sights, sounds, and smells, and comfortable with the comings and goings of people.

A hobby breeder might or might not accept your application for one of their puppies. Remember that they are not breeding to make money. They have a serious, long-term investment in their breeding program and every puppy they produce is precious to them. Most hobby breeders will expect you to sign a contract, in which they will lay out what they expect of you in your care of the puppy they have so lovingly raised, and what you may expect of them. A good hobby breeder's contract will include a statement that they will take their puppy back at any point in its life should you no longer be able to or want to keep it.

If you are accepted, the breeder will keep your hopes and goals in mind every day as she watches the puppies from birth, and will offer you the one, or possibly a choice of two puppies, who she thinks will be the best match for you. You might find the undersized female adorable, for example, but the breeder is thinking about your entire life with the dog, and knows from her experience that this puppy will always be too small and delicate for the active hiking and running life you have outlined as your ideal. Once you have chosen a hobby breeder, trust her judgment. She has as great a stake in the success of this placement as you do.

Finding a hobby breeder isn't difficult. Most hobby breeders are affiliated with breed, performance, or sport clubs. Examples of breed registration organizations are the Australian Shepherd Club of America, The United Kennel Club, the American Kennel Club (AKC), and the American Rare Breed Association, all of which maintain lists of breeders affiliated with their groups.

Many breeders sign a Code of Ethics when they join their organization. They follow strict rules of conduct in their breeding practices. However, it is important that you research your prospective breeder(s) to ensure that you are comfortable with their practices, from ethical considerations to practical puppy-raising. Contact any breeder whose dog breeds you are interested in. Start with a conversation, learn about each other, visit in person or over Skype if you can. Sometimes it may be possible to go see dogs a particular breeder has produced at dog shows. By prior arrangement, you might be able to talk to the breeder there as well — but be sure you do make prior arrangements, and do not approach her until she has finished in the ring.

Hobby breeders do not breed their dogs often, and their puppies can be expensive. A hobby breeder's breeding program is a very important part of their lives, not a profitable business. These breeders invest a great deal in each litter of puppies. Expenses include top quality food for mother and pups, vaccinations, health screenings, enrichment for the growing puppies, and much more. The cost of your puppy covers most or occasionally all of those expenses. Hobby breeders seldom make any profit on their litters. Any money they do make goes back into the breeding program.

Hobby breeders usually have only one or two litters a year at most, and often every puppy is already spoken for by someone who has been on the breeder's waiting list for some time. So don't expect to bring home a puppy from your first meeting with a hobby breeder. Be willing to wait for the right puppy, or for a space on the breeders waiting list to open up.

The wait and price will be worth it, though. If you find the right hobby breeder, you will have lifelong educated support from her and a strong, sound, properly-started puppy that will truly become your dream dog.

Dixie Tenny

11 Other Recommended Sources for Puppies

If you are looking for a mixed-breed puppy, or want to explore different sources for a purebred pup, here are some options to consider:

Rescue groups

Most breeds have their own rescue organizations. These are run by people who know and love that particular breed and are willing to dedicate time and energy to finding new homes for unwanted or abandoned dogs of that breed. There are national, state, regional, and local breed rescues. The best way to find them is to go to a search engine and enter "rescue" and the name of the breed you are looking for, plus any additional information you want to include. Example: "Oregon English Springer Spaniel rescue".

Besides rescues for individual breeds, you can also find rescues for groups of similar breeds, such as rescues for sighthounds or herding breeds. Some areas have umbrella groups such as Seattle Purebred Dog Rescue, Inc., which handle many breeds of dogs through connections to individual "breed representatives" or single-breed rescues. These umbrella groups play the middleman between you and the breed of dog you want, and can be very helpful if there isn't a particular breed rescue close to you. There are also rescue groups who handle puppies and dogs by area or region, regardless of whether they are purebred or mixed-breed. These can be excellent sources for puppies.

With any rescue organization, be prepared to fill out paperwork, to be interviewed, to ask and be asked many questions. Rescuers take their stewardship of homeless dogs very seriously These dogs have already lost one home (or more), and they want to be very certain that the new home each dog goes into has the best possible chance of being its best and last. There will be a contract to sign, outlining your responsibilities to the dog and the organization's responsibilities to you. You'll also need to pay an adoption fee or donation for a rescue dog. Most rescuers are volunteers and their efforts are supported largely, sometimes completely, by donations.

Will rescues have purebred puppies? Rarely, because the majority of rescued dogs are adolescents and adults. But it does happen. If you want a puppy only, make that clear up front and ask how often puppies come into that organization. Of course there can be no guarantee — a rescue group might handle three litters one year and none the next. Breed and region play a part in that: a German Shepherd rescue might respond that they do get some puppies in every year, while a Lakeland Terrier rescue might tell you they often don't even get one adult dog per year, let alone a puppy. Different parts of the country see overflows and scarcities in different breeds, at different times.

It's also helpful to be clear about what you mean by the word "puppy." While I consider that puppyhood ends at 16-18 weeks when dogs become adolescents, many people use the term much more loosely to refer to animals less than a year old, sometimes even older depending on when that particular breed matures. If you want a puppy between 8-12 weeks of age, you need to say that.

Thoroughly check out any rescue you plan to work with. They range from excellent to appalling in their practices. Anyone can collect animals and call herself a rescue organization. Even a well-meaning or widely recognized rescue group, when inundated with puppies and dogs, can lose sight of the importance of making the right match. Look for a professionally operated and well-run group, with a clean facility or foster homes, with dogs who look healthy and respond well to you, ideally connected to a breed club or some other parent organization. Look up references and check them.

Vet offices and hospitals

Another source for puppies is your veterinarian or animal hospital. Clients often contact their veterinarians for help finding good new homes for pets they cannot keep. If you make your veterinarian aware of what you are looking for, he or she can direct owners of likely prospects to you if any occur. Most of these will be adult dogs, but sometimes a family member proves to be allergic to a new puppy, or well-meaning adult children give a puppy to an elderly parent who does not want or need a young puppy in her life.

Neighbors/farm dogs/yard signs/flyers

When I was a child in the 1960s, almost everyone I knew got their dogs this way. Spaying and neutering was not common and dogs often ran the neighborhoods with their children, so litters happened fairly frequently. These days it is rare to run across a litter of puppies playing in someone's yard, because of the success of the movement to spay and neuter pet dogs. But occasionally a friend's or neighbor's dog has a litter, or a "puppies for sale" sign can still be seen on a drive in the country. Some people put up fliers on community bulletin boards in churches, restaurants, or coffee shops advertising available puppies from a "surprise" litter.

These "accidental" puppies need careful evaluation, but many can become great pets. If the mother and father both have good friendly temperaments, the mother is well cared for during her pregnancy and while she is nursing, if the puppies are raised underfoot in the house where they experience the sights, sounds, and smells of everyday life and get lovingly handled, they may well turn out to be fine pet dogs.

But take care that you do not exchange your *dream puppy* for the *most convenient puppy*. It can be hard to say no when a neighbor, friend, or family member is hoping you will take one of their puppies. But if the litter parents are big, active dogs and your dream is to have a cuddly lap warmer, proceed with caution. Always remember you are making a choice for the next 15 years of your life, not just for the few months of puppyhood. Choose the puppy that will grow into the adult dog you truly want.

Animal shelters

Shelters might get puppies often, or very seldom. It depends on the area where the shelter's animals come from. Shelters rarely get purebred puppies. When they do, they are almost always either an unwanted gift or the "leftovers" from an unintentional or backyard breeding.

You're much more likely to find mixed breed puppies in shelters than purebreds. However, with the highly effective spay/neuter program in the United States, many shelters don't even get mixed breed puppies often. Talk to your local shelters, tell them what you are looking for, and ask

How to Find Your Dream Dog

how often they would expect such a puppy in their facility. Some shelters have waiting lists and will contact you if a puppy or dog of a type you are looking for comes in. With most, though, you will have to keep walking through and checking regularly.

With all of these options, remember to keep your guidelines for what you want firmly in mind. All puppies are cute, but you are looking for your dream dog.

12 Puppy Sources to Avoid

The sources in the last two chapters are all good places to look for a new puppy. But I also need to tell you about two places never to look for one: **puppy mills** and **pet shops.**

So-called "puppy mills," or commercial breeders, are the opposite of hobby breeders. They produce puppies for one reason only: to make money. And in order to make the greatest amount of profit, they breed as many dogs as possible and spend as little money and effort as possible on those dogs.

The adult dogs in puppy mills are fed cheap food, kept in bare, filthy cages, and forced to breed every time a female comes into season. They are not groomed, not exercised, given a minimum of medical care, and handled only when necessary. All adult dogs capable of breeding are bred, regardless of whether they are cripplingly shy, aggressive, or suffer from medical conditions that they can pass along to their pups.

Puppy mill puppies receive none of the handling and socializing so vital to normal puppy development. They are sold off as young as possible. They arrive at their destinations as cute as any other puppies, but they are ticking time bombs of medical and temperament problems likely to come.

In short, a puppy mill environment is a torturous life for its adult breeding dogs and the worst possible start for puppies. Puppy mills flood the market with unsafe, unsocialized, unhealthy, and unready puppies, very few of which will ever be good pets. *Do not buy from them.* Patronizing puppy mills is supporting animal cruelty and profiteering, and getting a puppy from that environment will be a traumatic experience both for you and for the dog.

Pet shops have been the traditional destination of puppy mill puppies for many years. Regardless of what the public may hear, **any puppy you see in a pet shop came from a puppy mill.** Responsible hobby breeders personally interview every potential owner of one of their puppies, to ensure that each carefully raised pup gets placed into the home where both owner and dog are most likely to be happy together throughout their lives. Pet shops have no such evaluation process, either for owners or dogs, so hobby breeders avoid them—but puppy mill owners love them, for the exact same reason. **Please avoid pet shop puppies at all cost.** The easiest way is to simply never enter a pet shop that sells puppies.

How do you know if you're looking at a puppy mill puppy? As the public has become more educated about avoiding puppy mills, these cash crop breeders have become more sly and clever about avoiding easy identification. You might encounter them for sale directly from the breeding facility, or through pet shops, or listed on the internet or in newspaper advertisements. They often to go great lengths to appear to be just a regular family with a litter, to try to fool the public into buying puppies from them.

Here are ways to be sure you do not accidentally buy a puppy mill puppy:

1. If the "breeder" does not interview you but is simply willing to take your money and hand you a puppy.

2. If the "breeder" refuses to allow you to visit his facility ("home") — usually offering the "convenience" of meeting you somewhere to exchange money for puppy.

3. If you cannot meet the mother of the litter.

4. If an ad or website lists more than two breeds available, especially - but not always - small breeds (there are a

very few good hobby breeders who produce more than two breeds.)

5. If the list includes mixed breeds disguised as purebreds, with made- up names combining the breeds in the mix, such as cavipoo, chi-tese, yorkidoodle, etc. (I have no ob- jection to mixed breeds, but an ad listing several breeds that includes these indicates a puppy mill that is trying to cash in on the fad for "designer dogs.")

6. If an online advertisement shows individual puppies with prices attached (even showing individual puppies with no prices attached is a red flag; hobby breeders do not want potential buyers to come see a litter with their heart already set on a particular puppy that might not be the right one for them.)

7. If a breeder takes your payment via credit card online.

If *any one of these* is true, you have almost certainly unmasked a puppy mill.

You may feel as if you want to "save" one of these puppies. Please think again. Buying from puppy mills contributes to the miserable, hopeless lives of the parent dogs and the production of puppies as if they were assembly-line products without any quality control. Owners who have succumbed to these feelings of compassion have reported incidents such as losing a five-month-old Golden Retriever to crippling hip dysplasia, spending thousands of dollars on skin conditions that cannot be cured, experiencing aggressive biting in a twelve-week-old puppy, and more. It's not worth it.

Ensuring that your puppy had a great start to life with a happy and healthy mother, good basic care, and loving socialization with humans is the ideal path to life with a dream dog. Make sure you look for yours in places that can and will confirm they operate this way—and nowhere else.

13 How do I choose my dream puppy?

Once you've found a good source for your puppy, the next issue is choosing the puppy itself.

If you are buying a pup from a hobby breeder, trust her to guide you in selecting the ideal puppy for you. Remember that she has been watching, caring for, and handling these puppies many times every single day since the moment of their birth, while you have only seen the litter occasionally, maybe even just once. And as a hobby breeder, she has as great a stake in the success of her puppy placements as you have in finding your perfect puppy. Every puppy she places

How to Find Your Dream Dog

carries her "kennel name" and represents the type of dog she produces to the public.

In general, make use of the knowledge of anyone who has been watching and caring for a litter of puppies you are interested in. Many experienced rescue individuals and foster homes can help you choose a puppy whose temperament they feel will be the best fit for you.

But occasionally you will be offered a choice between two or more puppies. Or, if you get your pup from a shelter, a friend's or neighbor's litter, a rescue litter, or another similar source, you might need to select your puppy without a breeder's or puppy-raiser's guidance. How do you evaluate the differences between individual puppies?

One of the very best ways to start evaluating a litter of puppies is to interact with their mother. In fact, this is so important that if the mother is in the home or facility but you are not allowed to meet her, that almost certainly means there's a problem the breeder doesn't want you to see. If that happens, walk away then and there. Don't buy from a breeder who won't let you meet the mother of the litter.

The mother has an enormous amount of influence over how her puppies turn out. She not only contributes 50% of their genes, she sets the example for them of how a dog should behave. In research, normal puppies placed with a shy mother dog as newborns become shy themselves as they grew. *So if you do not like the mother dog, if you do not feel you would be very happy if your puppy ended up like her, do not take home one of her puppies.*

Once you've met the mother (if possible—in shelters and rescues it may not be), you can start meeting the puppies. If you can, visit when the puppies have awakened from a nap, eaten a meal, and are ready to play. Do the puppies look healthy, bright-eyed, and busy? If the litter looks unhealthy, look elsewhere for your dream dog. Don't imagine that a condition such as a skin rash, diarrhea, vomiting, or lethargy will necessarily clear up once you get a puppy home. Some never do. There are few things as tragic as acquiring an adorable puppy who is ill, and watching it get steadily sicker and eventually die.

If the litter in general seems fine but there is one puppy who is very quiet, stays in a corner, and/or rejects all the other puppies' attempts to play with it, do not choose that puppy. At worst, it may be ill, but even at best, that is not the normal cheerful temperament that we want to see in healthy puppies. Don't be tempted into thinking this is just a "quiet" puppy that will grow into a "quiet" dog. Physically and behaviorally healthy puppies are active during playtime.

To get to know the different puppies, sit on the floor in the middle of the puppy group and watch all the interactions. Ask the breeder for some of the puppies' toys. Always have one in your hand, and offer it to mouthy puppies so they won't chew on your skin. Stroke with one hand while the pup is engaged with the toy in your other hand. Stay until

How to Find Your Dream Dog

the puppies are winding down and looking for places to curl up and sleep.

Remember that puppies, during play, practice all the skills they would need if they were going to grow up without the care of humans. The instinct to rehearse every part of the stalk-chase-kill prey cycle is present in all puppies, whether they are Alaskan Malamutes or Pekingese. Normal behaviors that you are likely to see include:

- Puppies playing, sometimes very roughly, with barking and the occasional yelp.

- Lots of running and chasing.

- Tug games with toys, with growling.

- Shaking soft toys violently (to "kill" them).

- Tearing toys apart.

- Chewing on each other.

- Mounting each other.

- Biting each other.

- Stopping play suddenly to get a drink, to urinate, or to poop.

Observe which puppies approach you and which do not. Look for human attachment behavior, such as a pup bringing a toy onto your lap and settling down to chew it, or lying against your hip, however briefly. A puppy who is already inclined to seek out the company of humans has excellent potential to become a great pet dog. A puppy who shows little or no interest may become a fine pet, too, but getting and keeping this pup's attention may be more of a challenge than the one who offers attention freely.

As the puppies start to slow down just a bit, gently pick up each puppy and see how they react to being held. It's normal for them to be a bit squirmy. But which puppies look up at your face? Be sure you are smiling and your eyes are soft so you don't intimidate them.

You can also get up and walk around a bit (shuffle, so as not to step on anyone). Which pups are interested, and follow you? Which look but don't follow?

By the time the puppies start to tire and settle down to sleep, you will have started to see each one as an individual, with its own personality. While the boldest pup may have delighted you, or the shyest pup may have charmed you, it's the human attachment behaviors that are your best clue as to which puppy is most likely to become your dream dog.

So let's review. To evaluate and choose the right individual puppy, you are looking for:

1. A mother dog you love, if you are lucky enough to meet her

2. A puppy who is outgoing and playful, clearly healthy and happy

3. A puppy who is comfortable being handled

4. A puppy who actively engages with you, even for very short periods of time

All puppies are adorable. But it's very possible that none of the cute puppies in a particular litter will seem "just right" to you. Don't be afraid to say "thanks, but no thanks." There will be other litters to look at, and you will know when the puppy of your dreams appears. Do not compromise on something that will be so important to your life for a decade or longer. Choose the puppy that will become your dream dog.

One last thought on choosing a puppy. As you watched the litter play, did it start to become clear why it's such a challenge to raise a young puppy? Many of the behaviors of puppies that are normal for them are problematic for their humans. Puppies put their teeth on everything, just as young human babies at a certain stage put everything they pick up into their mouths. That isn't a problem when they have tough-skinned littermates to chew on, but once you bring a puppy home everything from the edge of the Oriental rug to the television cords to delicate human skin is a potential chew object. This need to bite and chew cannot be "corrected": it really is a need while a puppy is young. When the puppy outgrows that stage, it will stop by itself without any need for correction if it has been handled well during that stage.

An eight-week-old puppy needs to eat three times a day, drink many times a day, urinate up to 17 times a day, and poop at least four times a day, often more. It takes a tremendous amount of time and effort, patience, and consistency to get a young puppy through its babyhood and on its way to becoming your dream dog. The good news is that if you put in this time and effort, if you stay patient and consistent, by the time your puppy becomes an adolescent at 16-18 weeks of age, you will have set the best possible foundation for your dream dog's future. But if watching the energy and activity of the puppies made you think twice about bringing such a demanding young creature home, there is another great option.

Dixie Tenny

PART 4:
The Adult Dog Option

So, what if you have read this book and, considering your life carefully, you have realized that a puppy wouldn't be right for you right now—but that you would love to adopt an adult dog?

That's great! An adult or an adolescent dog can be an excellent alternative to a puppy. Many of the same considerations apply as with a puppy; it's important to choose the right dog that's a good fit for you and your household. But adopting an adult dog can be much easier than getting a puppy. Not only are many adult dogs already socialized with basic house manners, there are far more to choose from.

In today's hectic world, many owners who start out with the best of intentions find out that they are too busy to give a dog the time and attention it needs and deserves. But those owners' loss can be your gain—as well as your new adult dog's.

14 Pros and cons of adult vs. puppy

When you look at a puppy, you can only tell in the vaguest of terms what kind of dog it will grow into. As we've seen, getting a particular breed and buying or adopting from a reputable source can increase the chances of your new puppy growing into the dream dog you want, but there are no guarantees. There is a much greater degree of "what you see is what you get" with a dog who is already grown.

This is particularly true when you can observe the dog in a home environment, either its own original home or a foster home. Dogs do not thrive in shelter environments. Some dogs shut down, others are constantly agitated, jumping and barking. Some guard-type dogs, with no territory or people of their own in a shelter to guard, can even appear to be more easy-going than they will be when their new territory is established and they have bonded with their new people — and therefore have something to guard again. Talk to the shelter staff about any dog you are interested in, and spend as much time as possible in a "get- acquainted" area with the dog. Consider: if the dog never changed from what you are seeing today, would you want it? *Never adopt any dog assuming it will change, or that you can change it.* It might change. But it might not.

Many adult dogs arrive at their new homes house-trained and with good house manners. All normal adult dogs have far greater bladder and bowel control than any young puppy, so they will only need to go outside several times a day instead of very frequently. Most fully adult dogs will not be the compulsive chewers that puppies and most adolescent dogs are, either—though all dogs should have access to acceptable chew toys at all times.

Some adult dogs already walk nicely on leash, and may already know how to respond to some common cues such as "sit" and "down." Adult dogs have adult brains and adult attention spans, and with the right type of patient and kind training, can learn quickly and remember what they have learned. Physically mature dogs, after a vet check to determine their soundness, arrive ready to be walking and hiking companions or, if they're the right breed and in good condition, running partners.

The early socialization period for adult dogs is in the past. This can be good news or bad news, because either the dog was socialized as a puppy...or it wasn't. Assume that what you see is what you are always going to see. Do not expect to change a dog who is afraid of your children into a dog who loves them. If you have children or will be around them a lot, look for an easy-going dog who actively seeks them out, who responds to them with clear interest and warmth and a sweet nature.

Similarly, do not assume that a dog who does not appear to like other dogs will decide to like the dog you already have at home, or your adult daughter's dog that she brings to the house whenever she comes over. If a dog has no known history with cats, do not adopt it if you have cats. Many dogs are predatory toward smaller, fast-moving animals, and a dog with no cat experience—or who might have chased or even killed cats in its previous life—cannot be expected to be a safe household companion for your cat. Look for a dog who is living peaceably in a foster home or its original home together with cats.

Can an adult dog truly bond with a new owner? The answer is absolutely yes. Some of the dogs most closely bonded to their owners — police K9 corps, drug-sniffing dogs, guide dogs for the blind, wheelchair assistance dogs, and many more working dogs—do not meet their human partners until they are adult dogs. Some adult pet dogs will bond with their new owners immediately. Others will be too confused or worried for instant bonding, but will quickly respond to a new home with kind and fair rules, consistent behavior from the humans, a routine the dog can come to trust, and bond-enhancing activities such as playing, training, walking and exploring together.

In fact, a better question might be "can a young puppy truly bond with its new owner?" A very young human baby will let anyone warm and loving rock it, feed it, and hold it, until quite suddenly, it reaches an age where it knows who its family is and becomes wary, for a while, of anyone else. Puppies under the age of 16-18 weeks are similar. They can move from person to person and environment to environment with little if any stress or concern. It is when they cross into early adolescence at 16-18 weeks of age that they begin to see a difference between their family members and everyone else. That is when real bonding with individual people begins to occur.

So your dream dog might be an adult dog rather than a puppy. Adult dogs can be much easier to bring into your life than puppies. And their potential issues are usually easily solved by having realistic expectations, using common sense, and making sure the adult dog you choose is the right one for you.

15 Good Sources For Adult Dogs

Some of the same sources for puppies can be good sources for adult dogs as well. But there are also sources that seldom or never have available puppies, but almost always have adult and adolescent dogs available.

Guide Dog or Assistance Dog Organizations

You've probably seen guide dogs and assistance dogs out and about with owners who need special help and support. What you may not know is that many dogs who go through training to become service dogs like these don't graduate from the training program successfully. Standards of performance for assistance dogs are extremely high— and rightly so, considering that these dogs' future owners will depend on them in a way few of us ever have to depend on a dog.

Adolescent and young adult dogs who have gone through some or all of their advanced training but who will not be placed as assistance dogs are called "career change" dogs. These dogs are usually specially bred Labrador and Golden retrievers or a cross of those two breeds, plus, very occasionally, German Shepherds or Standard Poodles. All have been extensively socialized by puppy raisers up to approximately a year old. They have been taken on elevators, into shops and restaurants, sometimes even to baseball parks and on trains and airplanes. They have also been taught to respond to many cues, and have excellent manners at home and in public.

And not completing the training does not mean that these "career change" dogs are in any way badly-behaved or difficult. There are many reasons why a dog might not graduate from a service dog training program, including refusal to disobey its handler in dangerous situations (a guide dog must be willing to refuse to move forward into traffic even if its handler tells it to). These dogs are generally very well socialized and well trained, and make outstanding pets.

Equally outstanding are retired service dogs. These are dogs who have given years of service as assistance companions, but who can no longer do the demanding work that this job requires. Most of these dogs stay with their owners/ partners even after they can no longer work, but sometimes for various reasons that is not possible and the dog becomes available for adoption.

If Labs and Goldens appeal to you, career change dogs and retired service dogs are an unparalleled source of thoroughly socialized and well-trained pet dogs. There are always waiting lists for them. Contact both national and local accredited guide and service dog organizations for details.

Hobby breeders/breed rescues/breed club contacts

Hobby breeders are not just for puppies! Sometimes these breeders have to make hard choices about which of their dogs to keep and which to make available to pet homes. A typical hobby breeder might have two very promising young adult show prospects but only room in her home to keep one of them. Or she might choose to place a retired champion whose breeding career is over up for adoption, so the dog can spend the rest of his life enjoying "only dog" privileges. These dogs are not advertised, because the breeder is willing to take as long as necessary to find the ideal home for each of her dogs. If adopting an adult dog this way interests you, talk to breeders at dog shows (*after* they are finished showing in the ring, when they have the time to talk). Or contact national or local breed club secretaries to find out if there are available adult dogs in that breed.

How to Find Your Dream Dog

Breed rescues are organizations devoted to locating, fostering, caring for, and placing unwanted dogs of particular breeds. Almost every national breed club has a rescue coordinator who keeps track of available dogs, their locations and histories. There are also many local and regional rescue groups for particular breeds. Most of the dogs handled by breed rescue groups are adults.

Rescue groups and shelters

As noted earlier, most available dogs in rescue groups and in shelters are adolescents and adults. Many adolescents are given up for adoption for nothing more than being normal, untrained adolescent dogs. As puppies they were small, cute, and easy to manage, but as they grew and were not managed well or trained, their original owners no longer enjoyed living with them. So they were given to a rescue group or shelter to place.

Fully adult dogs are given up for adoption for reasons ranging from behavioral issues (some serious, such as aggression or severe shyness; some, again, simply stemming from a lack of guidance or training) to death of the owner, to bizarre reasons such as "doesn't match my new carpet" or "rolls on my new sod." Many are strays with unknown histories. Keep your "dream dog" firmly in mind if you visit a shelter or a rescue group, or scroll through the dogs on Petfinder or another online listing of available rescue dogs.

Veterinarians

Clients often contact a trusted veterinarian to help them find homes for dogs they can no longer keep. Again, reasons vary widely. In this case, as well as interviewing the owner about the dog and, with luck, meeting it in its original home, you can also confirm with the veterinarian that the dog is physically and behaviorally healthy and sound. Veterinarians can be an excellent source for well-loved and cared-for dogs whose owners must find new homes for them.

Neighbors, friends, family

It's also possible, though less common, to adopt a dog that a neighbor or friend is unable to keep. Many people, when they find they can't keep a beloved pet any more, talk first to people they know. If you can step in and take the dog yourself, you will not only get a dog you already know and like, you'll be a lifesaver for your friend, who now has peace of mind that their dog will go to a home they trust.

How to Find Your Dream Dog

CONCLUSION
What Next?

In this book, you've learned everything you need to know in order to find and adopt your dream dog. You've determined whether you're really ready, examined your reasons for adopting, and learned what puppies are like and what they need from you. You've explored some of the different qualities of puppies and dogs that might make them great pets for you (or not). You've found out where to find puppies and where not to even look. And you've considered the differences between puppies and adult dogs, in case an adolescent or adult is a better choice for you than a puppy right now. You're prepared to welcome an amazing puppy or dog into your life.

Before you head out and start looking for that dream dog, I've got two last questions for you to think about:

What if, after considering all of this, I run across a dog totally different from the one I had in mind and fall in love with it?

Of course you can change your mind if you like — it's your dream dog, after all. But if you have considered yourself and your lifestyle carefully and made some important choices that felt right to you, pause and think hard before applying to adopt a dog who is a very different type from the one you felt would suit you best.

A Rough Collie in full coat can be a breath-taking dog, magnificent-looking and sweet-tempered, conjuring up visions of Lassie. But if you decided you did not want to bother with a lot of brushing and grooming, and that you wanted a small-to-medium sized, quiet dog, will you really be happy with a Rough Collie, no matter how beautiful? Unfortunately, Lassie was an actor, with a top professional trainer, and her behavior and adventures on television were fictional. Real collies have real-dog issues such as matting hair, a tendency to bark a lot, and a herding breed's need for regular physical and mental exercise - even when it's muddy outside.

This is why it's important to decide which dog is your dream dog before you go looking. To those of us who love dogs, they are all wonderful and dear and appealing. But as we've seen in these pages, dogs are very different from each other. Your dream dog is the one who is right for you, who will enhance your life and make you wonder how you ever lived without him or her.

What if there is no potential dream dog in the litter or shelter I'm looking at?

Not every litter of puppies contains one that can become your dream dog. Not every rescue or shelter or even hobby breeder will have a puppy or dog that is right for you.

If you are truly committed to finding your dream dog, you will not knowingly bring the wrong puppy or dog home.

Yes, that might mean walking out of a shelter without a dog. It might mean driving away from a rescue's foster home empty-handed even though the anxious foster "mom" really tried to convince you that this puppy or dog was right for you. It might mean having a serious conversation with a breeder you have been working with, explaining why something about the pup she thought was right for you is raising a red flag. In my case, it has meant flying home alone when the pup I contracted for halfway across the country, seen and approved by a friend & colleague, was not what I was looking for when I arrived in person to fly her home under my airplane seat. It has also meant driving five hours to pick up a much-wanted puppy, spending the night there at a hotel with the pup, and returning it to the breeder the next morning, driving five hours back to disappointed children.

If you don't trust yourself to walk away even though it might be necessary, bring a clear-eyed and practical-minded friend with you when you visit your prospective dog(s) or litters of puppies. Listen to them and trust their judgement.

It's not easy to make this choice. But please consider the decision in terms of your lifetime with the dog. If you find the strength to walk away, within a few weeks, months, or maybe a year, you will have found the right dog and will be settling into a happy and satisfying canine lifetime with it. If you bring the wrong one home, you are setting yourself up for a decade or more of stress and regret. Which is worse, disappointing your children by not bringing home an expected puppy, or having the only dog they will remember throughout their childhoods be vividly different from what you expect and hope for? Which is worse, losing money — even a few hundred dollars — wasting time and energy preparing for a puppy or dog you then choose not to adopt, or spending much, much more in fees to trainers to try to "correct" behaviors you brought home knowingly, even though you did not want them?

Remember, a shy puppy is likely to become a shy adult. A very pushy puppy is likely to be challenging to handle. A puppy who has little-to-no interest in you as a 7- or 8-week-old is unlikely to become the faithful and devoted companion you dream of as it ages. All of these pups have appropriate homes available for them, as long as their behavior is not too extreme, but those are *three different homes.* If one suits you, the others do not, and bringing one of those others home just because you feel pressured to (by a breeder, a rescue person, a shelter worker, your children, or your own mind) isn't doing you or the dog any favors. Remember that not only do you commit yourself to a possible fifteen years with the wrong dog if you make this move, *you are equally condemning the dog to spending its entire lifetime in a home that is not suited to it.*

Evaluating an individual puppy or dog, or an entire litter or group of dogs, does not mean choosing the one who most closely approximates what you are looking for. It means knowing what you are looking for, and not accepting anything less.

Wait for your dream dog. He, or she, is out there, or will be. Choose carefully and wisely, and stick to your decision once you make it. Both you and the dog will benefit from the right choice.

I wish you the best in your Dream Dog search!

FREQUENTLY ASKED QUESTIONS

What is the ideal age to adopt a puppy?

8-12 weeks is the ideal age range for puppy adoption, in most cases.

Younger than 8 weeks is seldom if ever a good idea. Younger puppies are very immature. They are still learning how to be dogs from their mother and littermates. If someone is trying to convince you to take a younger puppy, it is often because by five or six weeks the pups are active, need solid food, and are suddenly a lot of trouble for the person who is raising them to deal with. They are also very cute when they are very young. But I suggest looking elsewhere for a puppy if this is the case. The puppy will be a better adult dog if it gets to spend its first full seven weeks with its mother and littermates.

There will be times when a younger puppy is already separated from its mother at a younger age, such as when a young litter is brought to a shelter. If you do adopt a puppy younger than 8 weeks old, be prepared for a very immature baby who needs a great deal of sleep and rest and extremely short playtimes. You will need to find a way to make up for its loss of littermate and mother interaction time, by finding other young compatible puppies it can have short play periods with, and ideally at least one older dog who likes puppies for it to interact with. You will, of course, have a longer wait until the younger puppy's bladder and bowels are mature enough for it to last through the night.

Very young puppies are also at greater risk for diseases, so be very careful where you take this puppy.

From 12 to 15 weeks, there isn't much time left in the all-important socialization window. So be aware that you will have to put in extra time and energy making certain this puppy gets properly socialized. Also, avoid a puppy this age or older who shows fearfulness or a lack of interest in people. That might never improve.

After 16 weeks, the socialization window has closed. A "puppy" over 16 weeks of age is really a young adolescent dog. So if you are looking at a young adolescent dog in this age range, look for one whose breeder or family who raised it has already done much of the socializing for you, and one who is well on the way to being house trained.

The good news about a young adolescent is that it will sleep through the night much sooner than an 8-week-old puppy, and become house trained more quickly, if it has been given a good start by its caretakers. A slightly more mature pup has a longer attention span than a baby puppy and is quick to learn. This can be a good age to acquire a young dog if and only if its needs, including its socialization needs, have been well taken care of by whoever raised it through its young puppyhood.

Many hobby breeders keep more than one puppy from a litter to "grow them up" a few extra weeks or even months and see who is the better show and breeding prospect between a promising pair. Both puppies will be equally well socialized, since the breeder doesn't know which one she will choose to keep. The other will become available as a very nice pet. It's also possible that a family raising a litter, especially a family with kind and careful children, might have given so much individual attention to their puppies that getting a slightly older pup from them will work out fine.

However, if such a puppy spent the period from birth until 16 weeks or later only with its littermates and without much human socialization, you may find that new experiences are very challenging for this puppy. The extra time in its litter might have solidified its position as very pushy or very shy, and that may be its default position with other dogs for life. But even the older pup who bullies its littermates may be fearful with humans if it has had little contact with them, or may freeze with fear in new situations. In my opinion, only a very experienced dog owner should undertake the challenge of adopting an under-socialized older puppy.

Some breeders choose not to make their puppies available until 12 weeks or even 16 weeks. Many toy breeders make this choice because their young puppies are so very small and fragile. It is worth remembering that the socialization window is the same for tiny puppies as for medium-sized and large ones. Make sure you find out how much socialization the breeder took on. Did the breeder get her puppies out and about so that they could acclimate to the world? Did she separate them from each other for most of the time after they turned 8 weeks of age, so that they have learned to sleep alone, entertain themselves with chew toys, and be generally independent of their littermates and mother? Does the breeder have them well on their way to being house trained? If not, look elsewhere for a puppy.

We would like to get littermate puppies to keep each other company (or one for each child). Is that a good idea?

Acquiring littermate puppies is risky. Littermates, like human siblings, begin developing relationships with each other very early in life. If one of the littermates you adopt has become pushy with the other, and the second pup typically gives in to its more assertive brother or sister, those qualities will only intensify as the pups stay together and grow older. Neither will have the chance to balance out its personality, so that the pushier pup can learn to relax and the quieter one to assert herself a bit more.

Another concern is that the puppies have known each other all their lives and are only now meeting you. It is not uncommon for littermates to stay more focused on each other than they are on their owners. In particular, the less assertive of a pair will tend to look to its bolder sister or brother for direction rather than to its owner. Of course there are exceptions, littermate pairs who do fine all their lives together. However, adopting littermates is not recommended because of the risks outlined above.

Adopting two unrelated puppies is a better bet. They have no relationship-from-babyhood with each other, therefore they are more likely to work out a healthy adult relationship with each other and with their owners. But take care: if one puppy is challenging to raise, two more than doubles the difficulty. Taking two puppies out for socialization, separately so that they don't learn to be over-dependent on each other in public, is more than most people are willing to do. Frequent daily separation at home is vital, too, so that they learn to be independent and also so each develops a personal relationship with you. Two puppies to feed, to buy crates and equipment for, to play with and train…is a lot to deal with. Along with the idyllic vision of two cute puppies playing together, be sure you envision one puppy pooping on the floor and the other running through it before you get the chance to clean it up. It will happen.

A much better idea is to raise one puppy to be a lovely, well-mannered and affectionate older adolescent or young adult dog, who can then be a role model for a second pup that you bring home a year or two later.

Is it better to get a mixed breed or a purebred dog?

If dogs ran loose in large groups, as they used to in the US before the 1970s and still do in many parts of the world, there would be a strong advantage to adopting a mixed breed. The fastest and strongest, physically fittest and smartest male was the one to catch and breed with the female, producing generations of smart, fit pups. However, a vanishingly small number of mixed breed dogs in the US are produced that way in the 21st century.

Some mixed breeds are the products of deliberate breedings between two purebred dogs: labradoodles (Labrador retriever x poodle), goldendoodles (Golden retriever x poodle), puggles (pug x beagle), and cockapoos (cocker spaniel x poodle) are some examples. Accidental mixed breedings tend to be between neighboring dogs, since very few dogs are allowed to roam loose.

Because of the great success of the American spay/neuter movement, most pet dogs cannot breed. So when a rare intact male dog comes across an equally rare sexually available female and they breed, it's difficult to tell how their puppies will turn out. The parents might be behaviorally and physically healthy, but they might not. The pups will inherit their parents' genes and will be strongly influenced by their mother's temperament. If that temperament is shy or aggressive, and those genes include a tendency toward a condition such as hip dysplasia or Von Willebrands disease, some of those pups will almost certainly have those issues.

Purebreds are deliberately bred, which can be either good or bad. Puppy mills breed any purebreds they have, regardless of their genes or their temperaments, purely for profit and as often as possible. They may also deliberately or accidentally produce mixed breeds and offer them as "designer breeds" with names like schnauzerpoos and cavachons, with high price tags. Like all puppy mill puppies, pups from these breedings have a slim chance of being behaviorally and physically healthy.

Hobby breeders, on the other hand, breed to produce the best-quality dogs that they can. Some use complex computer programs to attempt to keep their dogs' genetic health as strong as possible, and all provide their mother dogs and puppies with the best care available. These puppies have a good chance of being behaviorally and physically healthy. However, the gene pool of every "pure breed" is, by definition, limited to other dogs of that same breed. Any German Shepherd is genetically much more similar to every other German Shepherd than it is to any Dalmatian. If a physical or behavioral condition appears frequently in that limited gene pool, it can spread to other dogs of that same breed. Diligent breeders screen for common health and soundness problems in their breeds, and do their very best not to breed individuals with these problems. But the limitations of a closed gene pool make it impossible to remove such problems completely.

So there isn't really a clear advantage between purebred and mixed breed dogs. If you can find a puppy from behaviorally and physically sound and healthy parents with good temperaments that has been cherished from birth and carefully raised, whether it is a mixed breed or a purebred, it has an excellent chance of becoming a fine pet.

Does a male or a female dog make a better pet?

Some breeds (not all) have temperament differences between males and females. If you are looking at a purebred, ask breed experts if there are differences in that particular breed. Some breeds have size differences between adult males and females, as well.

Overall, though, individual temperament matters much more than a puppy's sex. There are many sweet-natured and cuddly male dogs, and many independent and assertive female dogs. The reverse is also true. Unless you must, for one reason or another, don't limit yourself by deciding in advance that you only want a puppy of one particular sex. You might miss the real dream puppy in the litter.

What if I want my new puppy to become a therapy dog?

Choose the individual dog for this kind of work with even greater care than you'd use selecting a pet, ideally with the guidance of a therapy dog professional. Many dogs, even in very "friendly" breeds, don't want to greet strangers at a nursing home or be handled by children they don't know at schools. Be sure you aren't projecting your own desire to do therapy work onto an unenthusiastic dog. Only dogs who truly love the work should be performing therapy.

How to Find Your Dream Dog

RESOURCES

This book has a companion website, www.dreamdogcentral.com. It features a puppy blog, stories and tips, updates on the information in this book, and much more. Come visit!

These are what I consider to be the very best resources at the time of this writing.

Resources on Dog Breeds and Types

It isn't easy to find unbiased information about different types of dogs. People who breed or own one type often think it is the very best that there is, and may overlook qualities that could present problems for some owners.

My favorite book about dog breeds is The Atlas of Dog Breeds of the World, by Bonnie Wilcox and Chris Walkowicz. It is a huge volume with lots of pictures and descriptions of hundreds of dog breeds from around the world. Just be careful you don't get your heart set on one that is rare even in its native country, which may be very far from yours! There are other books that cover many breeds. It's a good idea to look through several, and see what the descriptions have in common, and where they differ.

Online, some breed club websites have glowing descriptions of their breeds that may ignore or gloss over what it's really like to live with one. Other sites are excellent. Beware of any descriptions that sound too good to be true; they almost certainly are. Look for balanced descriptions that list both the joys and the challenges of living with a particular breed or type of dog. The best sites for that tend to be sites run by breed rescue organizations. They want each dog they place to stay in its new home, so they are usually very clear about what you can expect. If you have specific questions about a breed that its rescue site doesn't answer, email them and ask.

Books About Raising Puppies

Life Skills for Puppies by Helen Zulch and Daniel Mills

Puppy Savvy by Barbara Shumannfang

The Puppy Whisperer by Paul Owens

Puppy Primer, by Brenda Scidmore & Patricia McConnell Ph. D

Taking Care Of Puppy Business by Gail Pivar & Leslie Nelson

Book for Grown-Ups About Dogs and Kids

Happy Kids, Happy Dogs by Barbara Shumannfang

Book for Children About Raising and Training Puppies

Puppy Training for Kids: Teaching Children the Responsibilities and Joys of Puppy Care, Training, and Companionship, by Colleen Pelar and Amber Johnson

Books About Adopting an Adult Dog

Love Has No Age Limit: Welcoming an Adopted Dog into Your Home, by Patricia McConnell Ph. D and Karen B. London Ph. D

Successful Dog Adoptions, by Sue Sternberg

Book About Housetraining for Puppies and Adult Dogs

Way to Go! How to Housetrain a Dog of Any Age, by Karen B. London Ph.D. and Patricia B. McConnell Ph.D

Books About Training, for Adult Dogs (and Puppies Too!)

Dog-Friendly Dog Training, by Andrea Arden

Family Friendly Dog Training: A Six Week Program for You and Your Dog, by Patricia B McConnell Ph.D. and Aimee M Moore

Informative Books About the Human-Dog Bond

The Other End of the Leash, by Patricia McConnell Ph. D

Bones Would Rain From the Sky, by Suzanne Clothier

Book About Puppy Stages and Development

Another Piece of the Puzzle: Puppy Development, by Pat Hastings and Erin Ann Rouse

Book About Evaluating The Structure of A Dog Who You Would Like to Live An Active Lifestyle

Structure in Action: The Makings of a Durable Dog, by Pat Hastings and Wendy E Wallace DVM cVA

DVD About Evaluating The Structure of Puppies

Puppy Puzzle - Evaluating Structural Quality, by Pat Hastings

Recommended YouTube channels

Puppy and Dog Training and Behavior

kikopup

Thefamilydog

Facebook group, wonderful for guiding you as you socialize your puppy

The Social Puppy Games 2.0

ACKNOWLEDGEMENTS

I want to thank the team at The Master Wordsmith for their guidance and all their work on my behalf, without which making this book would have been very difficult if not impossible. James Ranson, Tyler Wagner, Meg Sylvia, and Joe Brachocki, many thanks.

Working on the photos for this book with Lynn Terry of Lynn Terry Photography was a real pleasure. Thanks Lynn; I can't wait to work with you again.

Thanks to friends and colleagues who read the manuscript at different stages and made helpful and insightful comments that definitely improved the final version: Kama Brown, Cinder Wilkinson-Kenner, Dr. Celeste Walsen, Shane Whelan, Paul Lehmann, Lucy Bailey, and Tracy Buck, thank you. And many thanks to "beta testers" Michael and Kerry Whelan, who used an early draft of this book as a guide while making decisions about a puppy adoption and gave me invaluable practical feedback. The fact that they found the book helpful and are very happy with the puppy they chose was most encouraging.

Finally, thanks to dog expert extraordinaire Kay Laurence and my fellow students in her Intelligent Dog Trainer Course. My thoughts about and attitudes toward the partnership between dogs and their people have forever been changed — for the better, I hope — by what I have learned from you. And to Dr. Jesús Rosales-Ruiz, ever supportive of my learning and my projects.

ABOUT THE AUTHOR

Dixie Tenny has been helping people and their dogs find each other and form successful partnerships since the early 1980s. She founded Purebred Dog Rescue of Saint Louis in 1984, and co-founded Seattle Purebred Dog Rescue, Inc. in 1987. That organization received an award from the Seattle Humane Society, due to the fact that SPDR's help in placing the shelter's purebreds allowed many more mixed breeds to be placed successfully as well. Dixie received the Seattle Kennel Club's "Honor Our Own" award in 2001 for her work with SPDR. Twice, Dixie has received the Gaines Good Sportsmanship medal.

Dixie served as Director of Training for the Greater St. Louis Training Club, Inc. for five years, where she arranged and hosted seminars featuring Dr. Patricia McConnell, Sue Ailsby, Dr. Roger Abrantes, Nicole Wilde, and Leslie Nelson of Tails-U-Win. In 2003 she and another trainer founded Dogs Unleashed, LLC, through which she worked with a wide range of behavior and training issues. During this period, Dixie also served for several years as a Judge for the Dog Writers' Association of America annual awards.

Dixie is a longtime member of the Association of Professional Dog Trainers (APDT). In 2010, Dixie became a Certified Training Partner with the Karen Pryor Academy for Animal Training and Behavior. Dixie formed her own business, Human-Animal Learning Opportunities, LLC, (HALO) in 2013. HALO hosts seminars for dog trainers, and has featured respected animal researchers and trainers Dr. Jesús Rosales-Ruiz and Steve White. Dixie took Kay

Laurence's "Intelligent Dog Trainer Course" in 2012-2013 and has been profoundly influenced by Kay's work. Other influences include Ken Ramirez, Gail Fisher, and Dale Gordon (of Northwest Dog Training School).

Dixie has lived with many dogs over the years, both purebreds and mixed breeds. She has shown dogs in conformation and obedience trials, created and taught Tricks classes, and dabbled in agility, K9 nose work, earthdog performance, and rally obedience. While in Seattle, Dixie raised a Labrador puppy for Canine Companions for Independence, Inc., a noted service dog organization. Currently Dixie lives with a Beauceron, a Papillon, and four cats in St. Louis, Missouri. When not doing things related to animals, she reads widely, enjoys the company of her three grown children, follows English Premier League soccer, and travels the world.

Made in the USA
Middletown, DE
13 October 2016